Introduction

This book will teach you what to draw and how to draw it. Simply follow the steps, in order, to complete your picture.

There are six steps for every drawing, each adding a small amount of detail to your picture. The first step is drawn already to help you get started.

Featuring cars, cakes, critters and much more, you can learn to draw 60 beautiful pictures in this charming book.

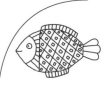

This book was completed by

....

Happy Hen

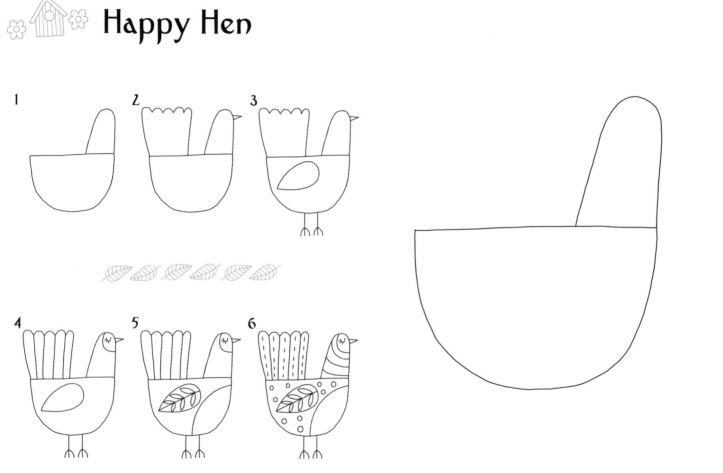

1

2

3

4

5

6

Flying Birdy

1

2

3

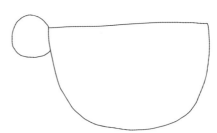

4

5

6

Yummy Cupcake

Delicious Cake

1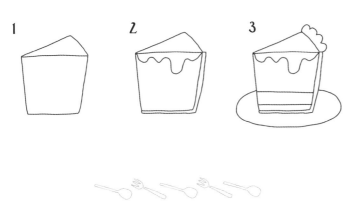

2

3

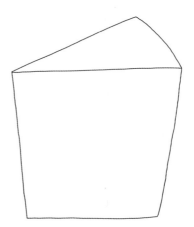

4

5

6

Beautiful Bouquet

1

2

3

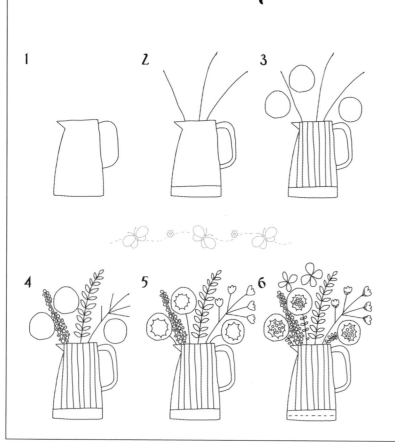

4

5

6

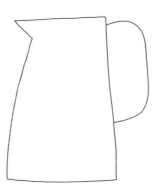

8

Pretty Petals

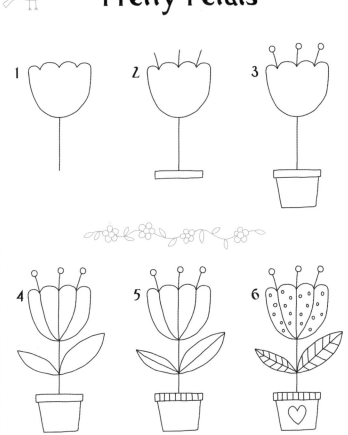

1
2
3
4
5
6

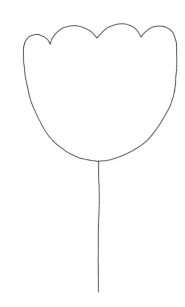

Super Helicopter

1

2

3

4

5

6

Amazing Aeroplane

1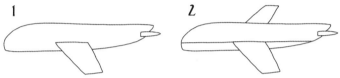

2

3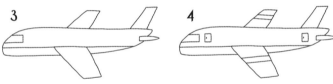

4

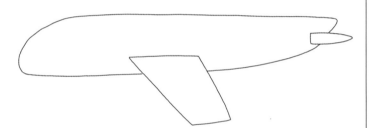

5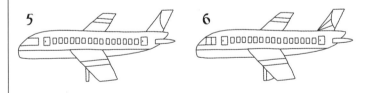

6

11

Cruise Ship

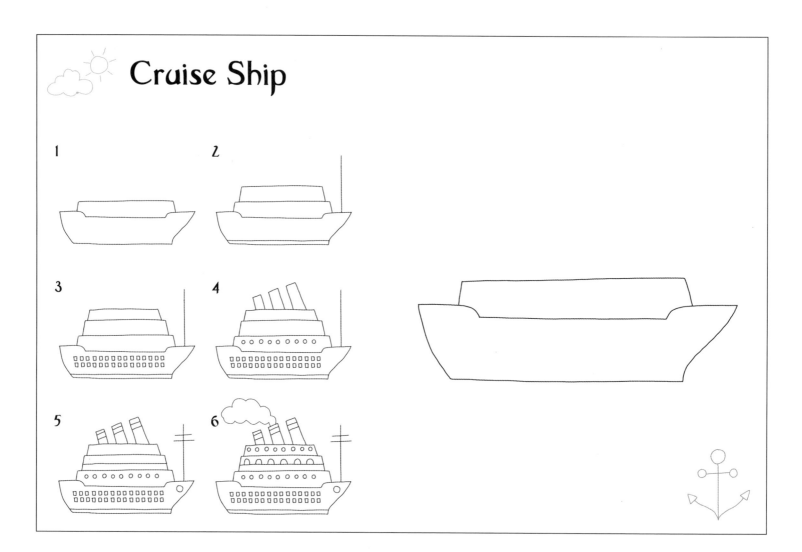

1

2

3

4

5

6

Fishing Boat

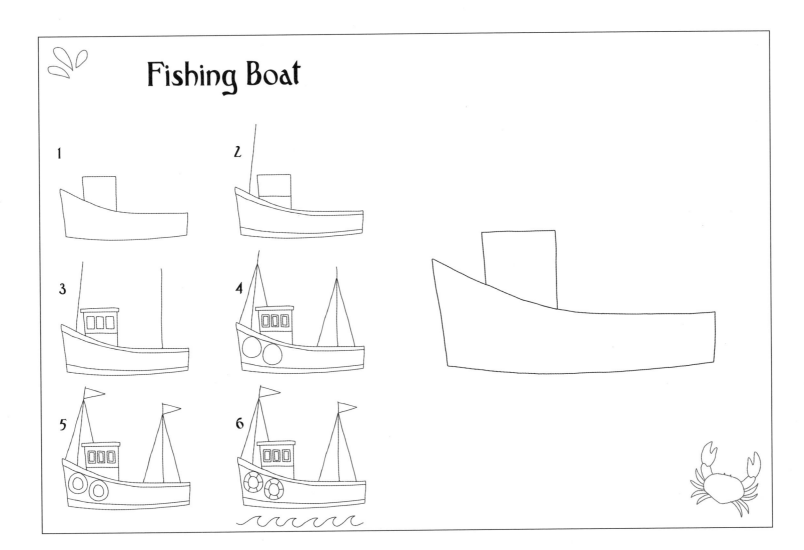

Jumping Grasshopper

1

2

3

4

5

6

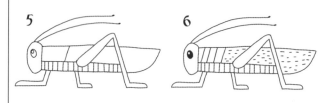

Busy Bee

1

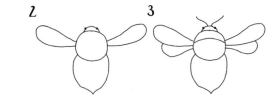

2

3

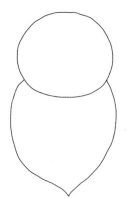

4

5

6

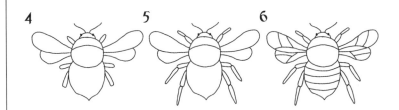

Home Sweet Home

1

2

3

4

5

6

Magnificent Palace

1

2

3

4

5

6

Fluttering Butterfly

1

2

3

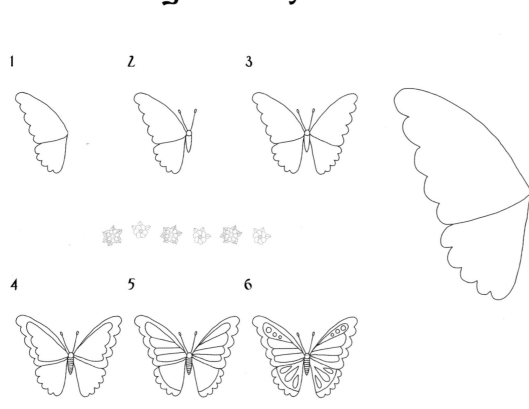

4

5

6

Beautiful Moth

1

2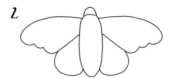

3

4

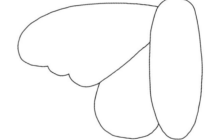

5

6

Playful Kitten

1

2

3

4

5

6

Purring Cat

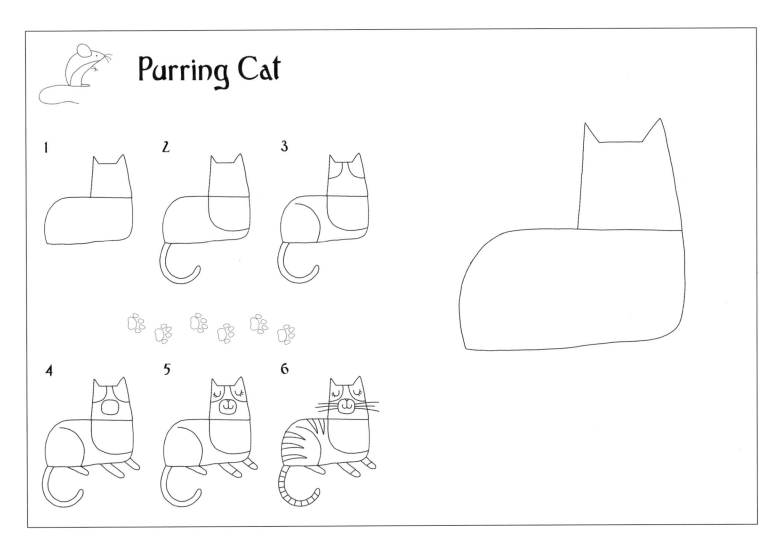

1

2

3

4

5

6

Tropical Turtle

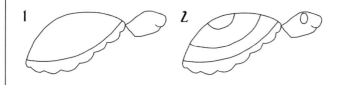

1

2

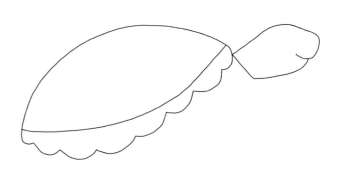

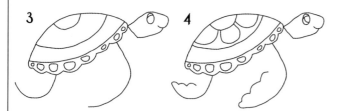

3

4

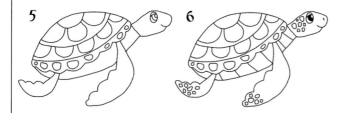

5

6

Lovely Lobster

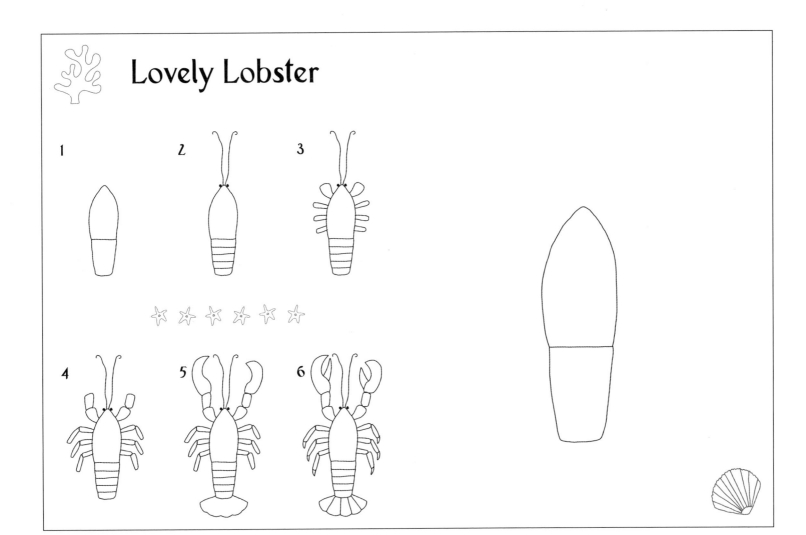

Curly Poodle

1

2

3

4

5

6

Cuddly Pug

1

2

3

4

5

6

Pretty Doll

1 2 3

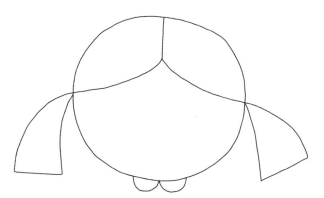

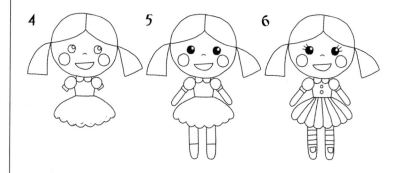

4 5 6

Russian Doll

1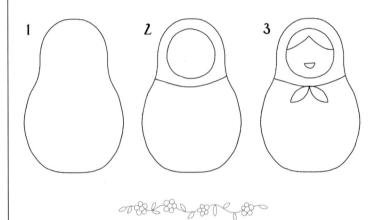

2

3

4

5

6

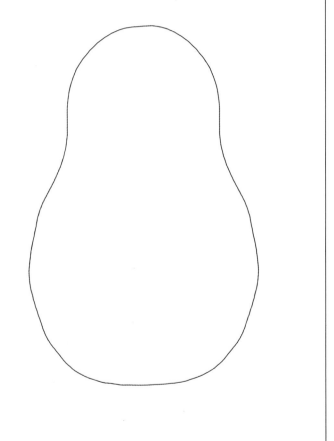

Fishy Friend

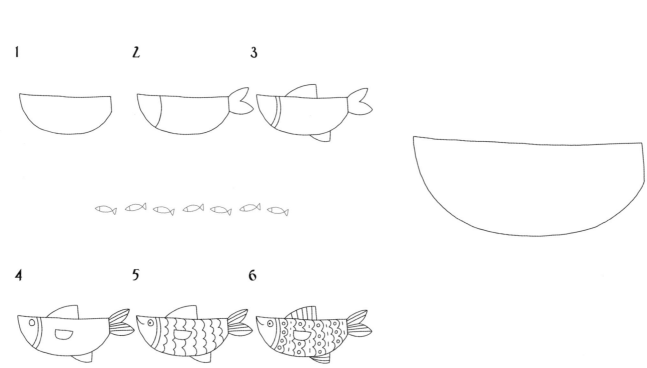

1

2

3

4

5

6

Fancy Fish

1   2   3

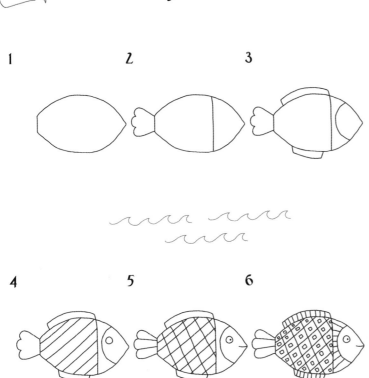

4   5   6

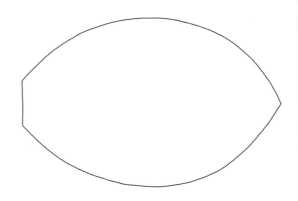

Pizza Party

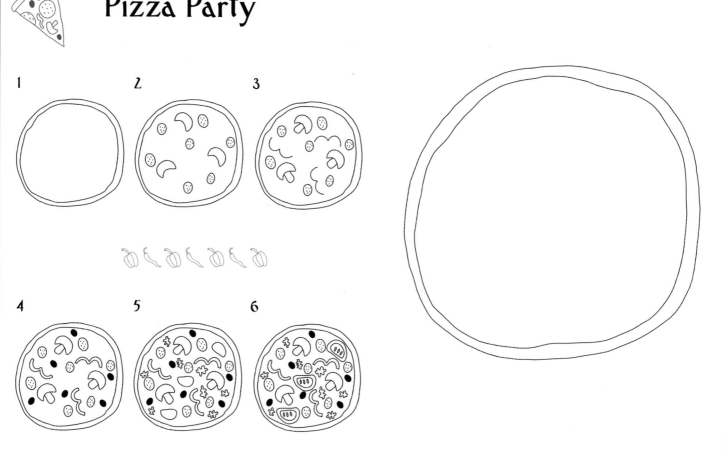

1

2

3

4

5

6

Burger and Chips

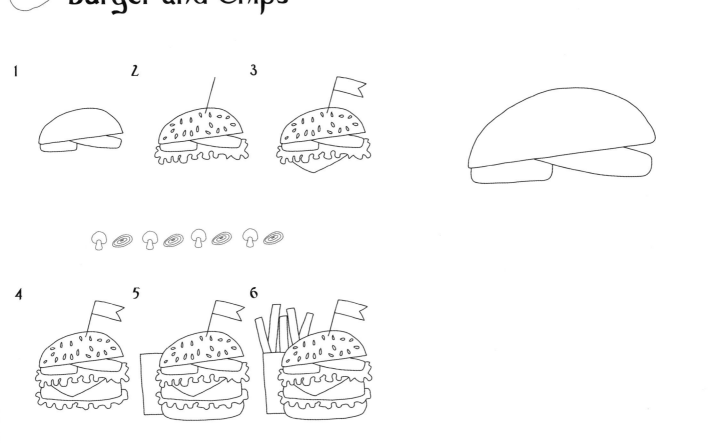

Happy Frog

1

2

3

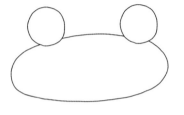

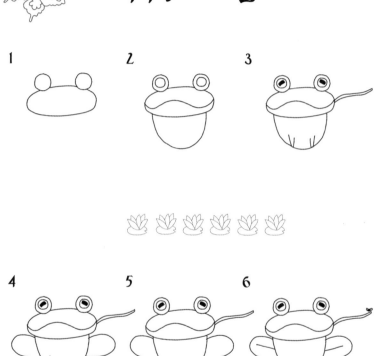

4

5

6

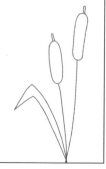

Grumpy Toad

1

2

3

4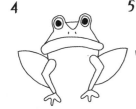

5

6

Chirpy Chicken

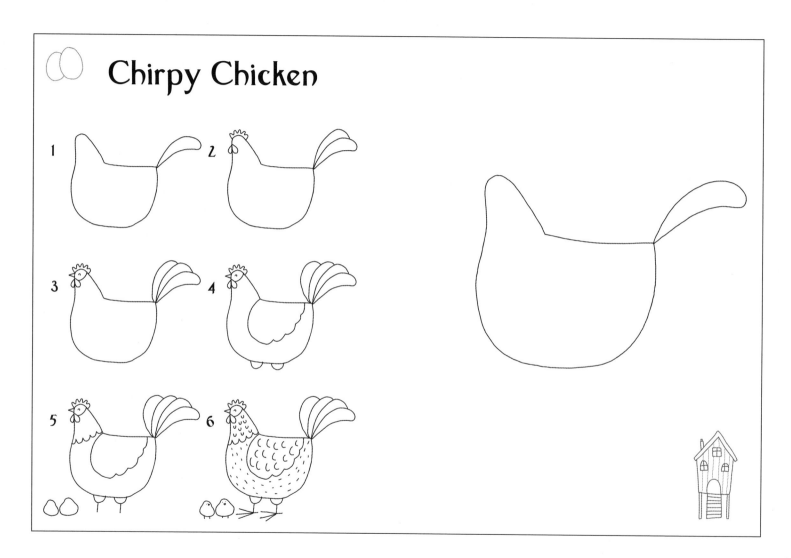

1

2

3

4

5

6

Crowing Rooster

1
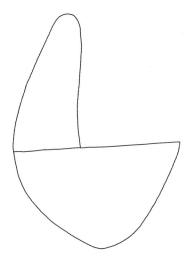

2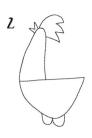

3

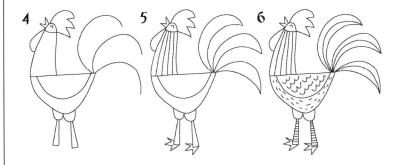
4   5   6

Ice Cream Sundae

1

2

3

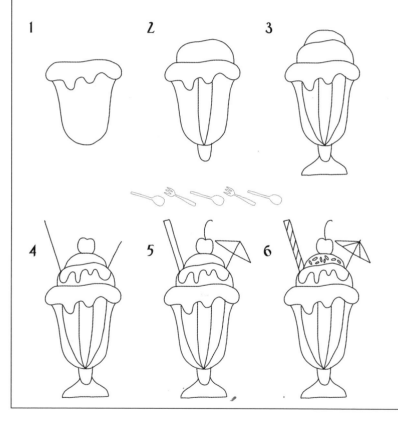

4

5

6

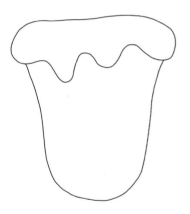

Berry Trifle

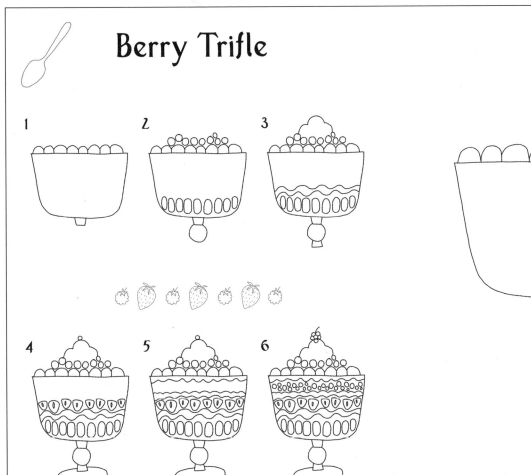

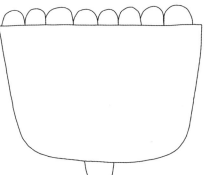

Beat of the Drum

1

2

3

4

5

6

Play Guitar

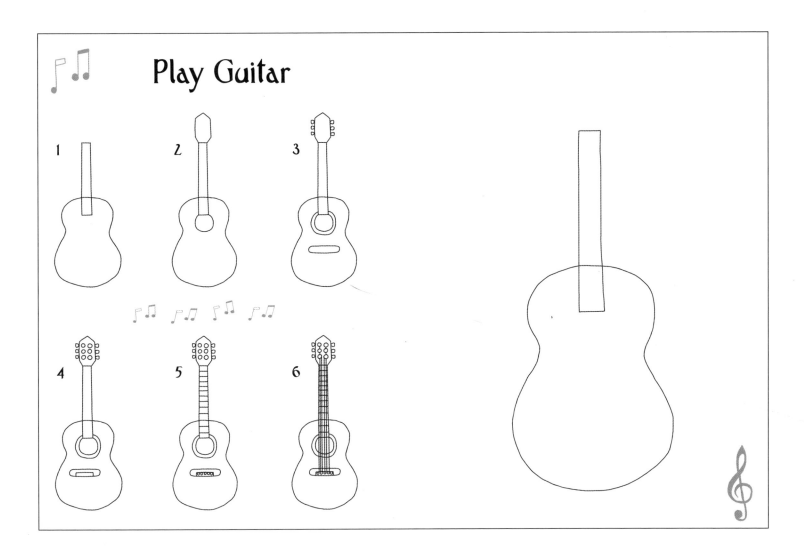

Hot air Balloon

Flying Kites

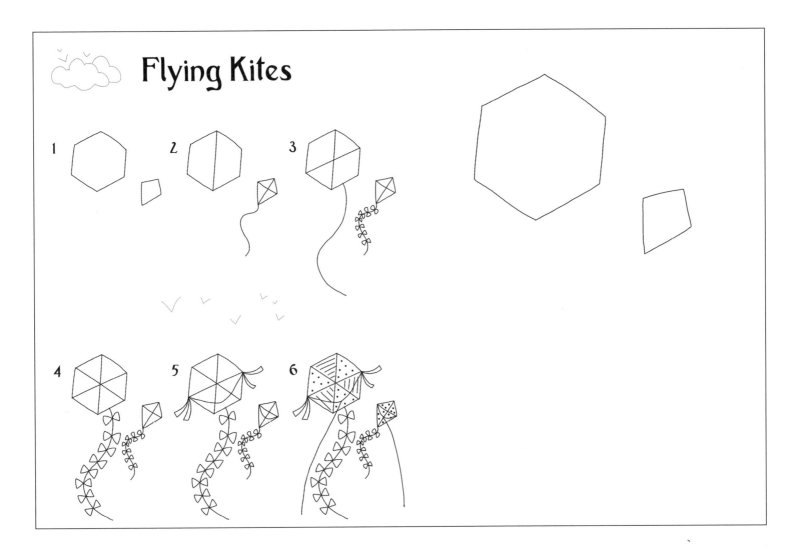

1

2

3

4

5

6

Enchanted Cottage

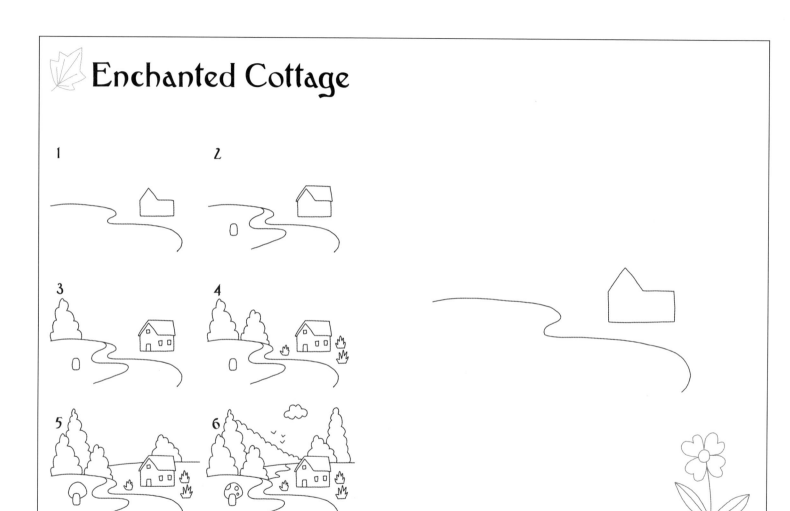

1

2

3

4

5

6

Magical Mountains

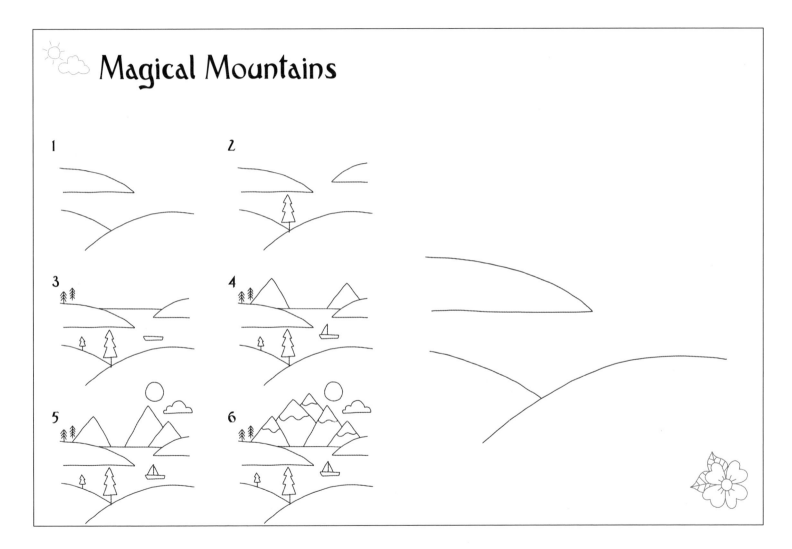

Friendly Lion

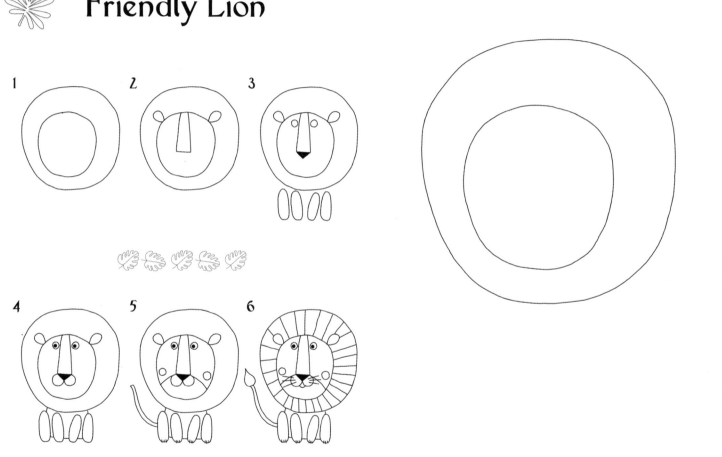

1

2

3

4

5

6

44

Sleepy Tiger

1
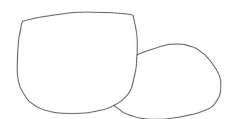

2

3

4

5

6

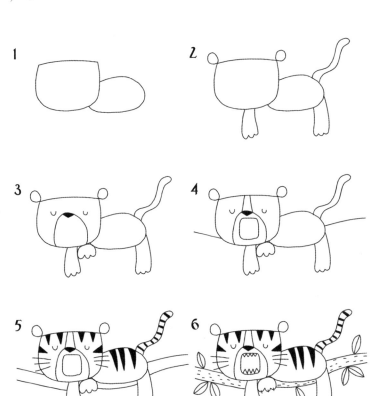

Swinging Orangutan

Big Baboon

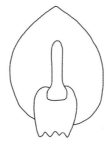

1

2

3

4

5

6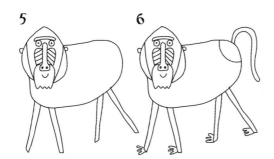

Terrific Toucan

1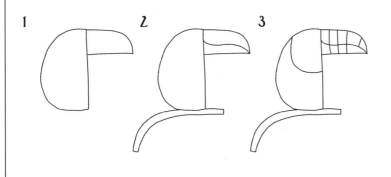

2

3

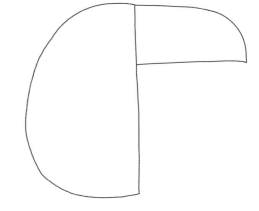

4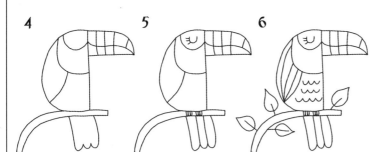

5

6

Talking Parrot

1

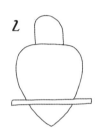

2

3

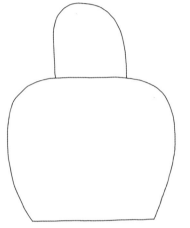

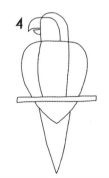

4

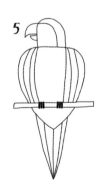

5

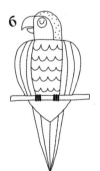

6

Muddy Pig

1

2

3

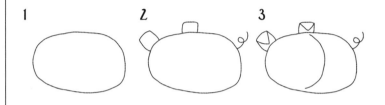

4

5

6

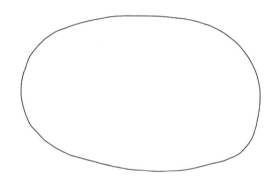

Hungry Cow

1

2

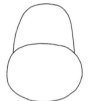

3

4

5

6

Lady

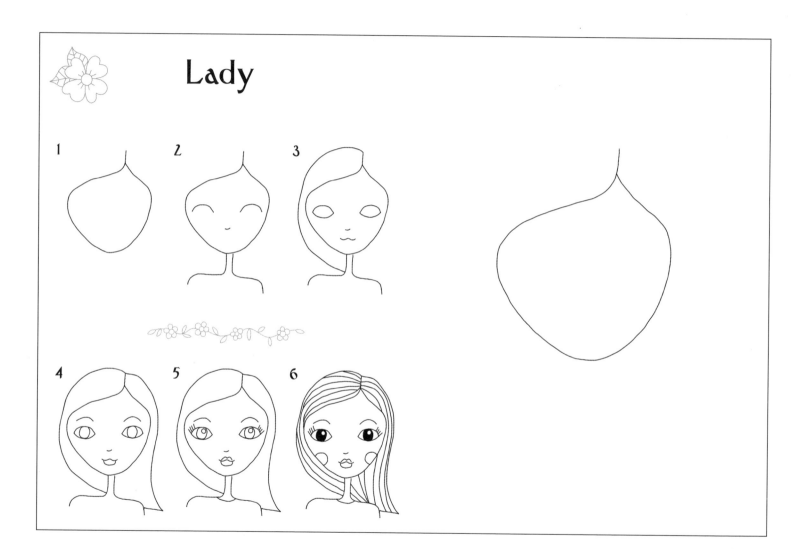

Gentleman

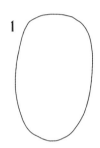

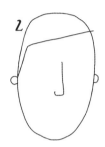

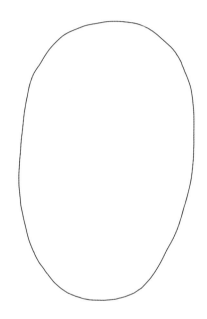

Fluffy Bunny

1

2

3

4

5

6

Running Rabbit

1

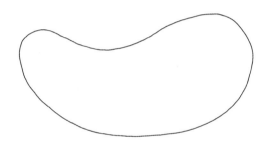

2

3

4

5

6

Trendy Trainers

1

2

3

4

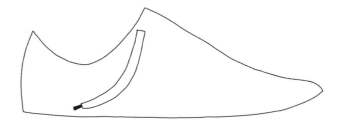

5

6

Shiny Shoes

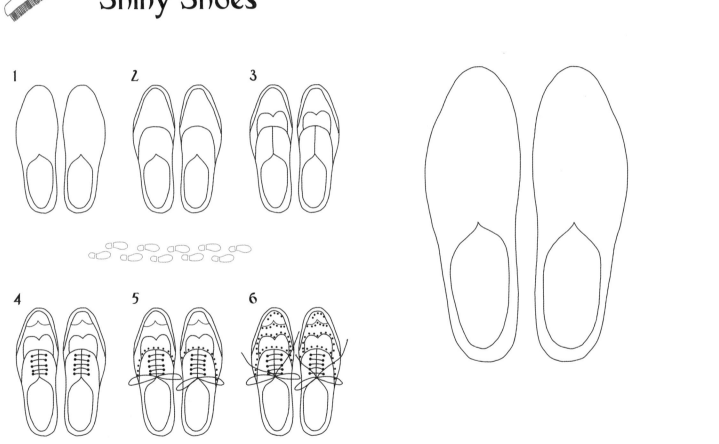

Gabbling Goose

Graceful Swan

1

2

3

4

5

6

Steam Train

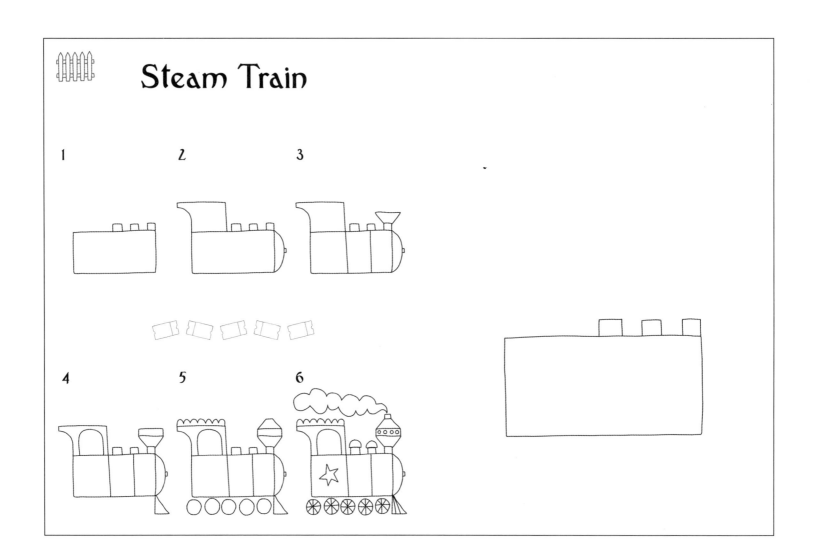

1

2

3

4

5

6

Model Train

1   2   3

4   5   6

Tropical Palm Tree

Apple Blossom Tree

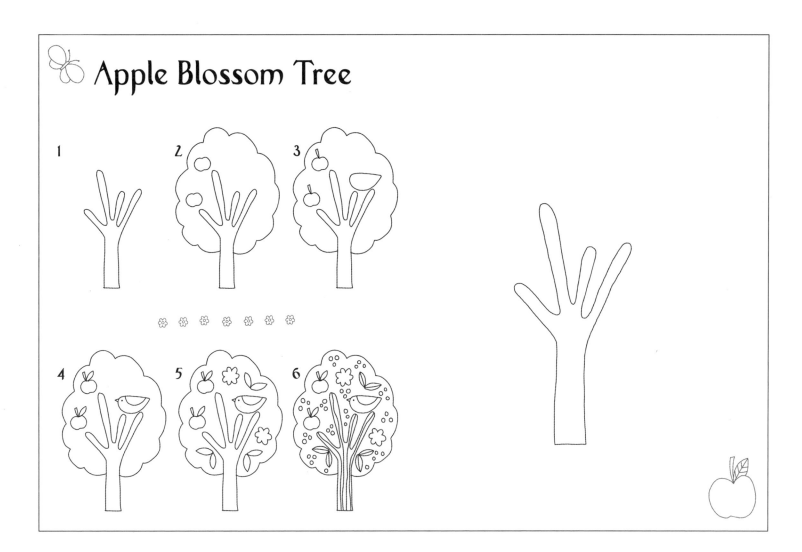

Illustrated by Charlotte Pepper
Edited by Lucienne O'Mara and Sophie Schrey
Designed by Derrian Bradder
Cover design by Angie Allison

First published in Great Britain in 2017 by
LOM Art, an imprint of Michael O'Mara Books Limited,
9 Lion Yard, Tremadoc Road, London SW4 7NQ

 www.mombooks.com/lom   Buster Books   @BusterBooks  @lomartbooks

A CIP catalogue record for this book is available from the British Library.

ISBN: 978-1-910552-71-1

3 5 7 9 10 8 6 4 2

This book was printed in December 2018 by Leo Paper Products Ltd, Heshan Astros Printing Limited, Xuantan Temple Industrial Zone, Gulao Town, Heshan City, Guangdong Province, China.